CAPTURED TELEVISION HISTORY

TV BRINGS BATTLE INTO THE HOME
WITH THE VIETNAM WAR

An Augmented Reading Experience

by Karen Latchana Kenney

Content Adviser: Alan Schroeder
Professor, School of Journalism
Northeastern University

COMPASS POINT BOOKS
a capstone imprint

Compass Point Books are published by Capstone Press,
1710 Roe Crest Drive, North Mankato, Minnesota 56003
www.mycapstone.com

Editorial Credits

Michelle Bisson, editor; Tracy McCabe, designer; Svetlana Zhurkin, media researcher;
Kathy McColley, production specialist; Library Consultant: Kathleen Baxter

Photo Credits

AP Photo: 29, 33, AP Corporate Archives, 37, Eddie Adams, 38; Getty Images:
Bettmann, 11, 21, 45, 52, 57, 59, CBS Photo Archive, 5, 6, 9, 24, 27, 31, 42, Corbis/
Nik Wheeler, 54, Hulton Archive, cover, 7, MPI, 26, Popperfoto/Rolls Press, 34; LBJ
Library: Cecil Stoughton, 23, 56 (bottom), 58, Frank Wolfe, 49, Yoichi Okamoto,
50, 51; Newscom: Everett Collection, 13, 14, 18, 25, 41, Universal Images Group/
Sovfoto, 46; Shutterstock: beibaoke, 56 (top); Svetlana Zhurkin, 55

Library of Congress Cataloging-in-Publication Data
Cataloging-in-publication information is on file with the Library of Congress.
ISBN 978-0-7565-5825-3 (library binding)
ISBN 978-0-7565-5829-1 (paperback)
ISBN 978-0-7565-5833-8 (ebook pdf)

Download the Capstone 4D app!

- Ask an adult to download the Capstone 4D app.

- Scan the cover and stars inside the book for additional content.

When you scan a spread, you'll find fun extra stuff
to go with this book! You can also find these things
on the web at www.capstone4D.com using the
password: Vietnam.58253

TABLEOFCONTENTS

Chapter One

DESTROYING CAM NE

It was August 5, 1965, and just as on any other night, Americans across the country tuned in to the *CBS Evening News* from their living rooms. Trusted anchorman Walter Cronkite hosted this daily 30-minute black-and-white television news program. From his desk in a busy newsroom, with various machines running and the *clickety-clack* of typewriters in the background, Cronkite welcomed viewers with his steady voice and strong presence. Besides reporting the world news, he introduced segments from CBS news correspondents—television reporters broadcasting from the field. Tonight was no different, but the segment was unlike any seen before. The footage was from the Vietnam War, a war raging in Southeast Asia that dominated the news. The correspondent was 33-year-old Morley Safer.

The segment brought viewers straight to the rice paddies surrounding a complex of rural villages called Cam Ne, south of the city of Da Nang in South Vietnam. The U.S. military believed that the Viet Cong occupied the villages. Mostly teenage boys and young men, the Viet Cong were guerrilla soldiers who fought differently from conventional troops. They formed smaller groups that made surprise attacks and used the villages as military bases. A treaty after World War II

Morley Safer's report from Cam Ne changed the way many in the United States thought of the Vietnam War.

(1939–1945) had split Vietnam into two countries—a democratic South Vietnam and a communist North Vietnam. The Viet Cong forces wanted South and North Vietnam to unite as one communist country. But the U.S. government did not want a communist Vietnam, and that's why the U.S. military was there.

On August 3, the day documented in Safer's report, U.S. troops were on a search-and-destroy mission to root out the hidden communists they

believed to be in Cam Ne. The marines walked in a single line ahead of Safer, his Vietnamese cameraman Ha Thuc Can, and a soundman named Thien. The three men were tethered together by an electrical cord linking their bulky camera, sound equipment, and battery pack. They traveled across a field with lush mountains in the distance and then reached the first village. Mud-and-reed huts topped by thatched grass roofs lined its mud alleys. The camera rolled, capturing a U.S. marine walk to a hut, lift his arm up, and calmly light a villager's home

SEARCH AND DESTROY

Members of the U.S. 173rd Airborne Brigade set off on a search-and-destroy mission in 1966.

The Viet Cong were difficult for the U.S. military to find. They infiltrated small rural villages in the area known as the Iron Triangle of South Vietnam. Many didn't wear uniforms and blended in with the villagers, who often gave them food and supplies, or became new recruits or a labor force to their army. To combat this hidden enemy, the U.S. military adopted a strategy called "search and destroy." The goal was to deny Viet Cong soldiers the villagers' support and their bases of operation so that they had to keep moving.

On a search-and-destroy mission, U.S. soldiers were dropped by helicopter into the thick jungles and waterlogged rice paddies. They entered villages by foot searching for Viet Cong soldiers and extra supplies, such as rice or weapons. Many times, the U.S. soldiers would set the villages on fire so that the Viet Cong could not use the buildings. They would also destroy crops or

food supplies, or take them away for redistribution. And they would try to kill as many suspected Viet Cong as they could, killing or injuring many civilians in their attempts. Then the soldiers forced the villagers to move to strategic hamlets, which were government camps surrounded by barbed wire and bamboo poles. The hamlets held concentrated groups of peasants, who could be protected by the South Vietnamese army and removed from Viet Cong influences.

But the search-and-destroy strategy and the Strategic Hamlet Program disrupted many villagers' lives. They began to resent U.S. soldiers and the South Vietnamese government. The villagers did not want to leave their homes and ancestral lands to live in the hamlets, and these tactics may have pushed many to join forces with the communist North Vietnamese.

on fire using his Zippo lighter. Other marines used flamethrowers, a kind of gun that projects a steady stream of fire. Every home in sight was ablaze as flames licked the sky above them.

Vietnamese villagers were seen stumbling out of their homes, crying and shouting. They were women, children, and elderly men—no young men or Viet Cong soldiers were in sight. The villagers were unarmed and did not fight against the marines. Then an elderly man pleads with Safer in Vietnamese, signaling to a hut being consumed by flames. Safer reports in front of the man, "This is what the war in Vietnam is all about: the old and the very young. The marines have burned this old couple's cottage because fire was coming from here. And now when you walk into the village you see no young people at all. . . . And the people that are left are like this woman here—the very old." The woman Safer refers to is elderly. She's trying to save some of her belongings from the fire, moving them into the trees.

Then the camera pans to a group of crying women and children, clinging to each other on the ground. Their faces are twisted in pain and agony as they watch their homes and all that they own disappear before them. Safer speaks over the footage: "If there were Viet Cong in the [villages], they were long gone, alerted by the roar of the amphibious tractors and heavy barrage of rocket fire laid down before the

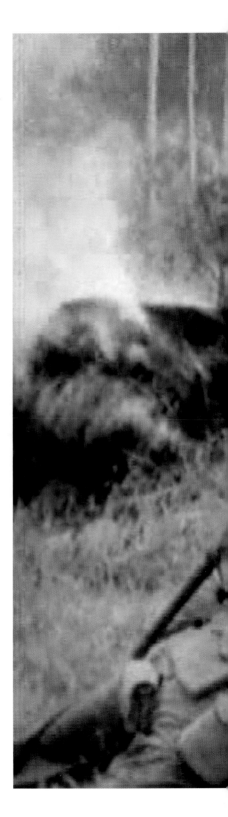

The homes of innocent villagers in Cam Ne were destroyed by U.S. troops trying to find Viet Cong.

troops moved in. The women and the old men who remained will never forget that August afternoon. The day's operation burned down 150 houses, wounded three women, killed one baby, wounded one marine, and netted these four prisoners—four old men who could not answer questions put to them in English."

On-screen, big, strong marines lead thin, elderly Vietnamese men who are blindfolded. They hold their arms up high, quietly surrendering to the soldiers.

The solemn segment concludes with Safer's thoughts on the day's operation. It was obvious that the United States had superior weaponry in the fight against the Viet Cong, he said, but it wasn't so clear how the marines were helping the Vietnamese people that day. Armed marines completely destroyed the innocent villagers' meager belongings. Their homes and few possessions were all that they had accumulated over a lifetime of hard labor. Land owned by families for generations had to be abandoned. The United States was supposed to be in the country to help the South Vietnamese people fight against the Viet Cong. But that day on television, it seemed that the marines were not on the South Vietnamese people's side at all.

Back in their living rooms, Americans were shocked by what they saw. Safer's segment revealed the U.S. military in a new light and exposed what

Back in their living rooms, Americans were shocked by what they saw.

Families watched the horrors of the Vietnam War on nightly news programs.

was really happening in the war. The marines were not simply the saviors of the South Vietnamese people, as many Americans had been told through the media—the U.S. presence in South Vietnam was harmful too. And the segment showed the true ugliness of war: real people were being harmed by the conflict and by the actions of U.S. troops. Women, children, and elderly civilians were now homeless because of that mission on one August day in Cam Ne.

ChapterTwo
A DIVIDED COUNTRY

Vietnam's problems weren't new in 1965. They started at least a few decades before U.S. soldiers arrived to fight in the war. Different foreign powers occupied the country throughout its long history—first China, then France, and finally Japan during World War II. After World War II ended and a defeated Japan left, France tried to retake control of Vietnam. But a new force was gaining strength—the Vietnamese people wanted to control their country. A revolutionary organization called the Viet Minh, led by communists and supported by the Soviet Union and China, fought the French and finally defeated them in 1954. The defeat led to a peace treaty, called the Geneva Accords, between France and the countries it had colonized: Vietnam, Cambodia, and Laos. Part of the agreement was that Vietnam would be temporarily split into two parts: the communist north and the U.S.-backed anticommunist south. According to the agreement, north and south would have an election in two years to choose one leader and unify the country. The Vietnamese people were independent from France, but their country was now divided. It would lead to an escalating conflict—one that the United States could not ignore.

The victorious Viet Minh marched into Hanoi in 1954.

Communism was the issue that most concerned the United States about Vietnam. The U.S. government saw its spread as a grave threat to democracy. Communist principles defied American ideals. In a communist country, wealth and goods are shared and the government controls wages, factories, farming, transportation, communication, and land. It's a society that seems the opposite of a capitalist one, like the United States, where individuals own land, factories, and companies. They compete to make money, and that competition is what many believe

makes America succeed. But communism was on
the rise in Eastern Europe, Asia, and other parts of
the world. To countries where many lived in poverty,
communism seemed to be a pathway to social equality.
First Russia turned to communism in the early 1920s,
becoming the Soviet Union. After World War II ended,
China became a communist state in 1949. Starting in
1950 North and South Korea became a communist
battleground during the Korean War (1950–1953).
While Russia and China supported the communist
North, the United States backed the South. And as

The U.S. government was afraid that communism was going to erase democracies around the world.

the Soviet Union and its Red Army gradually took control of countries in Eastern Europe, this growing superpower and China were supporting the spread of communism further into the west and into Asia.

The U.S. government was afraid that communism was going to erase democracies around the world. This fear led to the Cold War (1945–1991), a time of great tension between the Soviet Union and the United States. And then the Red Scare began in the United States in the late 1940s. During this period, many people were accused of being communists—and most were falsely accused. It was a damaging accusation. A communist was considered by many to be an enemy of the United States. Many employers questioned employees and fired those they thought were communists. People's names were published in books to warn the public of their supposed communist ties. The government also formed a committee to publicly investigate suspected communist activities, called the House un-American Activities Committee.

And just as these anticommunist feelings were at their height, television was catching on. This new technology became affordable to the average person right after World War II. Television brought the world to people's living rooms. Its earliest programs reflected the anticommunist feelings of U.S. society too. Television discussion programs, including one called *The Big Issue*, featured politicians talking about the evils of communism. In entertainment shows such as *The Man Called X*, U.S. spies gathered information about communists. TV became one of the public's major sources of world news too, through network news programs. By 1960 TV was fully woven into U.S. culture. It would soon be tested on the battlegrounds of the war brewing in Vietnam.

In 1960 the tension in Vietnam was growing. It was still divided. The 1956 election meant to unify the country never took place. The U.S.-backed leader of South Vietnam, Ngo Dinh Diem, refused to hold an election. The United States was determined to help Diem keep South Vietnam free from communism. In a 1954 news conference President Dwight D. Eisenhower explained why democracy was so important in Vietnam and its neighboring countries on the Indochinese peninsula: "You have broader considerations that might follow what you would call the 'falling domino' principle. You have a row of dominoes set up, you knock over the first one, and what will happen to the last one is the certainty that it will go over very quickly. So you could have a beginning of a disintegration that would have the most profound influences . . . with respect to more people passing under this domination, Asia, after all, has already lost some 450 million of its peoples to the Communist dictatorship, and we simply can't afford

By 1960 television was fully woven into U.S. culture. It would soon be tested on the battlegrounds of the war brewing in Vietnam.

greater losses . . . [which could lead to] the loss of Indochina, of Burma, of Thailand, of the Peninsula, and Indonesia . . ."

This described the U.S. government's domino theory—that if more Southeast Asian countries (including South Vietnam) became communist, nearby Southeast Asian neighbors would fall one after the other to communism too.

While the U.S. backed Diem's decision to stay independent from the North, not all of the South Vietnamese people did. The National Liberation Front (NLF) formed on December 20, 1960. Led by Ho Chi Minh, the NLF was a political organization that wanted to unify the two countries and was supported by North Vietnam, China, and the Soviet Union. The Viet Cong was the military group of the NLF.

As the NLF began to rise up against the South Vietnamese government, the United States became more and more involved. After John F. Kennedy became president in 1961, he sent increasing numbers of military advisers to assist the South Vietnamese army, called the Army of the Republic of Vietnam (ARVN), in its fight against the Viet Cong. The number of U.S. military personnel in Vietnam went from 900 in 1961 to 11,326 at the end of 1962, and to 16,000 in 1963. That number would just keep increasing, even after Diem's assassination on November 2, 1963, and Kennedy's assassination on

By the early 1960s, Vietnamese military were using U.S. aircraft to fight the Viet Cong.

November 22, 1963. Kennedy's successor, President Lyndon B. Johnson, would be the one to decide how involved the United States would get.

Johnson could remove U.S. military personnel from South Vietnam, but that would leave it wide open for a communist takeover. Or he could increase

> "We are very anxious to do what we can to help those people preserve their own freedom. We cherish ours and we would like to see them preserve theirs."

U.S. involvement in a war that seemed difficult to win. Both choices were bad for the United States. But, as had Kennedy, Johnson believed in the domino theory and spoke about America's duty to help South Vietnam fight off communism. In a televised interview called "A Conversation with the President," which aired on March 15, 1964, Johnson explained: "We are very anxious to do what we can to help those people preserve their own freedom. We cherish ours and we would like to see them preserve theirs. We have furnished them with counsel and advice, and men and materiel to help them in their attempts to defend themselves. If people would quit attacking them we'd have no problem, but for 10 years this problem has been going on."

In early August 1964 Johnson would make a decision about the level of U.S. involvement after an incident in the Gulf of Tonkin, a part of the South China Sea just off the coast of North Vietnam. On August 2 three North Vietnamese patrol torpedo (PT) boats fired at the USS *Maddox*, a Navy destroyer. The USS *Maddox* was struck by only one bullet but the PT boats did not fare as well. One sank and the others quickly returned to port. Government officials later believed that the PT boats had mistaken the USS *Maddox* for a South Vietnamese boat that had attacked them earlier. Then on August 4 another incident happened. It was a very stormy night and the

USS C. *Turner Joy* had joined the USS *Maddox* in the gulf. Radar and sonar operators on the USS *Maddox* thought they saw torpedoes coming toward the ship. They sent a radio message to the government that they were being attacked. Then they sent a second message saying that they weren't sure if they were being attacked. And they never saw an enemy boat in the water. Nevertheless, Johnson had made a decision. Whether or not they were real attacks, the Gulf of Tonkin incidents would set the U.S. involvement in the war in motion.

At 11:36 p.m. on the night of August 4 an important message from the president cut television viewers' commercial programs short. Johnson appeared at a podium between two U.S. flags, and slowly told the public about what had reportedly happened earlier that day in the Gulf of Tonkin. He explained how the U.S. was going to respond: "[the] renewed hostile actions against United States ships on the high seas in the Gulf of Tonkin have today required me to order the military forces of the United States to take action and reply. That reply is being given as I speak to you tonight. Air action is now in execution against certain supporting facilities in North Viet-Nam which have been used in these hostile operations. . . . I have today met with the leaders of both parties in the Congress of the United States and I have informed them that I shall

Whether or not they were real attacks, the Gulf of Tonkin incidents would set the U.S. involvement in the war in motion.

U.S. Navy carriers took part in the Gulf of Tonkin incident.

immediately request the Congress to pass a resolution making it clear that our Government is united in its determination to take all necessary measures in support of freedom and in defense of peace in southeast Asia."

The United States was bombing North Vietnam. It was the first direct U.S. action in the war. The resolution Johnson spoke about easily passed in Congress a few days later. It gave him the power to take any action he saw fit in Vietnam. Without officially declaring war, Johnson had sole power to take the United States to war. Few journalists at the time questioned Johnson's decision, and the public supported the fight against communists there. Johnson won the 1964 presidential election in a landslide. Just 18 days after his inauguration on January 20, 1965, he began sending troops to Vietnam. The United States was now actively engaged in the war, not just sending in advisers.

From the beginning, the war was televised on the nightly news. Media coverage of Vietnam was unlike coverage of previous wars. The military had provided much of the information about World War II and the Korean War to journalists. The military's footage showed positive images of the wars. American soldiers were doing good and always winning. It was highly produced, with music in the background and announcers reading scripts. As owners of the footage, the military could censor what was being shown to the public. And they did.

But when the Vietnam War began, television had been around for a while. Its technology was more advanced and mobile. Major television networks set up news bureaus in South Vietnam's capital of Saigon and kept crews of correspondents working day after day. Their reporters could go out into the conflict with cameras to film news stories. They did not need to rely on the military for footage. Their reports were

From the beginning, the war was televised.

In August 1964 President Johnson signed the Gulf of Tonkin resolution.

more spontaneous. As the war went on, the coverage was not highly produced. It did not have music or long descriptive narrations. It showed more raw footage of the harsh realities of war.

At first the coverage was upbeat, based on the journalists' daily military briefings. News anchors focused on victories and progress, like the reports from earlier wars. They'd do a battlefield roundup,

CBS News reporter Charles Collingwood walks through rubble in a section of Hanoi destroyed by U.S. troops.

telling how well Americans attacked the communists. One typical early CBS report, on August 23, 1965, showed Cronkite before a map of Southeast Asia. Over it was written "RED CHINA." Cronkite said, "American Air Force jets gave Communist Vietnamese their heaviest clobbering of the war today, hurling almost half a million pounds of explosives at targets in the North." The news showed

U.S. soldiers expertly using new military technology.
Viewers saw U.S. planes dropping bombs and troops
on patrol. The troops appeared brave and skilled,
easily handling the challenges of the war.

But the Vietnam War wasn't at all like previous
wars. There were no frontlines and few formal
battles. It was less clear who was winning or losing
or who was the hero or the enemy. Reporters soon
began showing the ugliness happening in the war.
Safer's Cam Ne black-and-white footage was one of
the first reports to show that the progress the military

announced wasn't so easy to see in the jungles and fields of Vietnam. Maybe that progress wasn't even happening.

Decades after the war, Bill Lenderking, a military officer who served in the Joint United States Public Affairs Office (JUSPAO), told about a military report that was simply false. His colleagues had been in the field early one day when a group of villagers surrendered to the U.S. military. They had been forced from their homes and were wandering without much food or water for several days. They were trying to survive. At the briefing that night, the official story was changed from the true events. Lenderking remembered, "At the end of the day I went to the five o'clock follies. And guess what they are talking about? The big news of the day, announced to a briefing room full of war correspondents, was this: a company or a platoon of 55 hard-core Viet Cong have come over to our side . . . this is what happens: an incident of some kind occurs, and immediately it is passed up the line, getting more distorted at each link in the chain." Lenderking knew those villagers were civilians, not Viet Cong soldiers. But that's not the story the JUSPAO wanted the correspondents to hear at the briefing that day.

THE FIVE O'CLOCK FOLLIES

Reporters in Vietnam attended the daily press briefings, but they didn't take them seriously.

Each day at around 5 o'clock, U.S. journalists gathered in Saigon's Rex Hotel. They were there to hear the official military briefings about the day's events. Presented by the Joint United States Public Affairs Office (JUSPAO), the briefings reported enemy body counts and victories in the field. The JUSPAO also handed out information packets containing the official military report. This information made it into the news and viewers' homes through journalists' and anchors' reports.

But the journalists, sometimes 400 to 500 in attendance, saw a different view of the war out in the field. The military reports did not match up. They were changed to create a positive image of the U.S. military. Journalists didn't trust these briefings and nicknamed them the "Five O'Clock Follies." It meant they saw the military briefings as a joke. Journalists openly questioned the news reported in the briefings and shouted at the officials.

THREE SCENES FROM THE WAR

Each day, U.S. viewers watched reports coming in from the Vietnam War. The body counts, the bombings, and the combat became part of daily life. Capturing that footage was a new challenge for correspondents. They caught rides with military helicopters and found themselves in the middle of combat. They looked for the "bang-bang" stories, as the networks called them. These stories showed action—soldiers shooting, planes bombing, and helicopters lifting the wounded to safety. It was what the networks wanted to put on the air.

On the afternoon of August 2, 1965, reporter Morley Safer was looking for an action story. He went around to different Marine Corps units near Da Nang looking to join up with a mission the next morning. Then he found a unit that told him, "Yes, we're going on a search-and-destroy in the morning. You want to come along?" Very early the next morning Safer, cameraman Ha Thuc Can, and soundman Thien joined the marines at a staging area by a creek close to the airport. Then they boarded amtracks: armored vehicles that could move through water. Safer didn't know much about the mission, so he asked a lieutenant. He told Safer, "We've had orders to take out this complex of villages called Cam Ne."

Morley Safer (right) joined a Marine Corps unit near Da Nang to capture ground combat in Vietnam.

Safer had never heard that before—to "take out" the villages. It sounded like Cam Ne was just going to be erased.

When the amtrack's ramp went down, Safer, Can, and Thien followed the first group of marines into the village. Their equipment and its cords linked them together. They had a 16 mm Auricon film camera and rolls of film, a battery pack, and other heavy equipment. Then the firing began. Suddenly a marine was down on Safer's right and a few more hit in front of them. They'd been shot in the buttocks and the back. Safer believed it was friendly fire—bullets from the marines, not enemy soldiers.

As Safer and his crew followed the soldiers into the village, they watched villagers running toward them and crying. They recorded the marines torching the villagers' homes. And when marines heard voices inside one hut, cameraman Can put down his camera and went to the doorway. People were hiding in a storage room beneath the dirt floor. Safer recalled, "'Wait,' [Can] says to the lieutenant. 'Please wait.' Standing in front of the ditch, in front of the flamethrower, he cups his hands and shouts in Vietnamese. 'Come out, come out now, and you will be safe. If you stay inside you will be killed.'" Cries from adults and a baby seeped out from the dark hut. Finally Can convinced the family to leave their home, and he picked up his camera again. Then he filmed their home erupting in flames.

Safer shipped his film and narration to the network headquarters in New York City. He sent the written story by telex, a system that sent text by telephone. After the story aired on August 5, people were outraged. Viewers called CBS, insisting that the story was a lie. The Defense Department told CBS News to remove Safer from Vietnam. The Marine Corps said the story had been faked. Even an angry President Johnson called CBS. He accused Safer of

U.S. Marines filed out of Cam Ne after burning down some 100 homes.

being a communist and said the report damaged the image of the U.S. CBS backed Safer, who was neither a communist nor a traitor. He was a journalist who happened to get a story that had an enormous effect on viewers. It was a fairly typical operation in the war.

South Vietnamese ARVN Rangers faced off against the Viet Cong in the the Tet Offensive.

The footage from the attacks showed chaos. The fighting had moved from the jungle to the streets of Saigon and other cities.

But it opened many people's eyes to the ugly nature of war and the role U.S. soldiers were playing in Vietnam.

Despite Safer's shocking report in August 1965, the war still had public support. News coverage throughout the next few years showed that the U.S. and ARVN were winning against the Viet Cong and the North. But the Viet Cong and the North were planning something big for the beginning of 1968. It would happen during Tet, the biggest holiday in Vietnam. During this three-day celebration of the new year, everyone took time off, even the South Vietnamese army. But during the holiday, on January 30 to 31, the North Vietnamese army and the Viet Cong simultaneously attacked major cities and populated areas across South Vietnam. They broke through the outer walls of the U.S. embassy in Saigon. It caught the United States and the South Vietnamese army by surprise. This was the Tet Offensive. The fighting went on for weeks, and many would die. Just two weeks after the fighting began, communist forces had suffered an estimated 39,000 casualties and democratic forces had 15,500 casualties. It showed that the Viet Cong were much tougher than the U.S. military had thought.

The footage from the attacks showed chaos. The fighting had moved from the jungle to the streets of Saigon and other cities. Journalists interviewed U.S. soldiers who were tired of the constant combat and of losing their friends. Everything seemed to be crumbling. The U.S. didn't appear to be winning the war at all.

And just after the attacks, another shocking TV segment aired in early February. It came from an NBC News crew that included reporter Howard Tuckner, cameramen Vo Huynh and Vo Suu, and soundman Le Phuc Dinh. And by chance an Associated Press photographer went along with them—Eddie Adams. The crew headed to the An Quang Pagoda, a Buddhist building thought to be a secret Viet Cong hospital, on the morning of February 1, 1968.

What the news crew caught on film was chilling. After a street battle, South Vietnamese officers captured a Viet Cong guerrilla soldier. He was barefoot and wearing a checked shirt and shorts. His hands were tied behind his back, and he had blood on his lips. The soldiers led him through the street up to Brigadier General Nguyen Ngoc Loan. Then Loan quietly walked up to the man, pulled out a gun, and shot him in the head. Loan turned around and walked away as the man fell to the ground. Blood spilled from his head. Tuckner made few comments, letting the footage speak for itself. He said, "Government troops had captured the commander of the Viet Cong commando unit. He was roughed up badly but refused to talk. A South Vietnamese officer held the pistol taken from the enemy officer. The chief of South

Then Loan quietly walked up to the man, pulled out a gun, and shot him in the head.

Vietnam's national police, Brigadier General Nguyen Ngoc Loan, was waiting for him."

NBC News played it as the lead story on the evening of February 2, 1968. Nearly 20 million people saw the report. Adams also took a photo that was printed in newspapers across the country the next morning. Viewers and readers did not know that the man who was executed, Nguyen Van Lem, was an assassin. He had just killed a police officer and his family, including children. They saw a man being casually shot and left to die on the street. The moment was brutal. The United States

A PULITZER PRIZE-WINNING PHOTO

This photo of a Viet Cong prisoner being shot became a rallying cry for antiwar protests.

The Associated Press reporter who tagged along with the NBC crew on February 1 was Eddie Adams. A chance photo that Adams took that day would change his life. Just as General Loan shot the Viet Cong prisoner, Adams' camera clicked. The black-and-white image he took captured the moment just before the man's death. It was horrifying and vivid. The photo showed the man's twisted expression just as the bullet hit his head. It showed soldiers watching and wincing at the shooting. And it showed General Loan with his gun just inches from the prisoner's head.

The photo became a symbol of the violence of the war. People held it up at antiwar protests. And, in 1969, it won Adams a Pulitzer Prize, the highest honor awarded to a journalist. The photo spread around the world, but Adams didn't ever want to speak about it. It hurt him to know how the photo affected General Loan's life and career. Adams was a former marine. He saw the shooting that day as just part of the war. He believed General Loan was doing his job. Adams never thought his photo deserved a Pulitzer Prize. He called it a "reflex photo," one he just happened to catch during one of many moments in the long war.

was supporting the South Vietnamese army. Many viewers wondered why. American men were dying there every day. Who were they helping? The footage showed a general coldly killing a man. The violence was nonstop and people were beginning to think the war was impossible to win.

There was more to the moment though—more than could be shown on a short television segment. General Loan was doing his job. He had been fighting against the Viet Cong for days during the Tet Offensive. He had just seen his best friend killed by a Viet Cong soldier. And Loan knew Lem had killed many people. He asked one of his soldiers to shoot Lem, but the man refused. So Loan later explained why he had to do it: "If you hesitate, if you didn't do your duty, the men won't follow you." But Loan's life changed after that. He became a symbol of the brutality of the Vietnam War. Many Americans hated him after they saw that moment caught on film.

The Viet Cong and the North thought the South Vietnamese people would join their side during the Tet Offensive. But the communists were wrong. The United States and ARVN won the battles and kept control of the cities. Yet the offensive showed that the war could not be easily won, as the U.S. government had been telling the public. The offensive began changing Americans' opinions. They were turning against the war. Just six days after the televised execution, Democratic New York Senator Robert

> "If you hesitate, if you didn't do your duty, the men won't follow you."

Kennedy gave a speech and said: "Last week a Viet Cong suspect was turned over to the Chief of the Vietnamese Security Services, who executed him on the spot. . . . Of course the enemy is brutal and cruel, and has done the same thing many times. But we are not fighting the Communists in order to become more like them—we fight to preserve our differences. The photograph of the execution was on front pages all around the world—leading our best and oldest friends to ask, more in sorrow than in anger, what has happened to America?"

In early 1968 senators, representatives, and others in the government were turning against President Johnson's decision to continue fighting the war in Vietnam.

After the Tet Offensive, CBS anchor Walter Cronkite went to Vietnam. Cronkite had supported the war in its early years. But his opinion started changing in 1967. He wanted to see the situation for himself. He later wrote, "The American public was utterly confused now because of the Tet offensive. The Viet Cong had risen. The North Vietnamese had gotten all the way down to Saigon." Cronkite wanted to "go out there and just try to bring perspective through one person's eyes." He made a few reports from the field and then CBS aired Cronkite's hour-long special on February 27. But it was far from just another news show.

"The photograph of the execution was on front pages all around the world—leading our best and oldest friends to ask, more in sorrow than in anger, what has happened to America?"

Democratic Senator Robert Kennedy, originally for the war, turned against it as the war continued.

Much of the report showed scenes from the field. It was straight reporting of the war. But at the end of the special, Cronkite added his personal thoughts about U.S. involvement in Vietnam. He told audiences: "It seems now more certain than ever, that the bloody experience of Vietnam is to end in a stalemate. To say that we are closer to victory today is to believe in the face of the evidence, the optimists who have been

Walter Cronkite's experiences in Vietnam changed his view of the war.

wrong in the past. . . . It is increasingly clear to this reporter that the only rational way out then will be to negotiate, not as victors, but as an honorable people who lived up to their pledge to defend democracy, and did the best they could."

Cronkite believed the war could not be won, and the United States needed to get out. Millions of Americans watched the *CBS Evening News*. It was the most watched news program of its time and Cronkite was the person entering Americans' living rooms every night. He was the most trusted anchorman on television, and his opinion mattered to those millions of viewers. Many thought Cronkite's Vietnam special changed how the public felt about the war. But Cronkite was modest about his influence, later saying, "I don't think I turned around public opinion on the war at all. I think . . . I was reflecting it."

ChapterFour
A TELEVISED WAR

The Tet Offensive was a turning point in the American public's support of the war. Television coverage during that time was mostly violent. The networks had plenty of dramatic "bang-bang" footage from this period. The fighting had left the jungles and rural areas of South Vietnam. It moved to cities and streets—to exposed areas where more typical kinds of fighting could occur. Tanks rolled through Saigon's streets. Soldiers shot at the enemy through abandoned high-rise buildings. They quickly ran through the streets avoiding sniper fire from above.

News stories highlighted the destruction caused by the fighting. Viewers saw cities in rubble and civilian casualties during Tet. The footage was raw and uncensored, unlike the footage of previous wars. They saw U.S. military casualties too. This violence, death, and destruction dominated the news in early 1968, much more than earlier coverage of the war. This extremely violent television coverage went on for two months. It was a bleak picture of the war. It seemed as if no side was winning—nothing seemed under control. American soldiers appeared to gain little during their violent battles. One NBC story, on February 20, 1968, showed this hopeless view of the war. It was from Hué, a large cultural city.

The fighting in Hué left much of the city in ruins.

The marines moved from house to house, trying to gain control of the city inch by inch. Reporter David Burrington said, "American marines are so bogged down in Hué that nobody will even predict when the battle will end. . . . More than 500 marines have been wounded and 100 killed since the fighting in Hué began. . . . The price has been high and it's gained about 50 yards a day or less in a heavily populated part of the citadel. Still, nothing is really secure . . ."

The devastating effect the war had on the Vietnamese people often went unreported.

Throughout the war, reporters had also covered many other kinds of stories. But they weren't the kinds of stories the networks wanted to run. They weren't exciting enough. Ron Steinman was the head of the NBC News bureau in Saigon during the war.

> **"They had little curiosity about how the average Vietnamese man lived his life and how a Vietnamese family coped when it lost a son in battle."**

He later wrote about his frustration with NBC's choice to mostly show action stories that "As bureau chief, I decided daily what we should cover. And, daily, [network] producers rejected almost every story about life in Vietnam. . . . They had little curiosity about how the average Vietnamese man lived his life and how a Vietnamese family coped when it lost a son in battle." And while television footage mostly showed fighting, Steinman wrote, "part of combat coverage is that often nothing happens. . . . Often [reporters] returned from the field believing the operation had been a bust. The platoon they covered had tramped through the jungle, did not find the enemy, and had come up empty." This was the Vietnam that television viewers never saw. It was also the war, but it never made it onto the nightly news.

But the Tet Offensive offered plenty of opportunities for action footage. It appeared as if the war would never end, but the United States and ARVN had actually won the battles and regained control of the cities. The Viet Cong and North Vietnamese soldiers fled back into hiding. Still, the heavy action and casualties shown on television had persuaded many Americans that the war could not be won. Public opinion had been changing for some time, though. Support for the war had been falling since 1966, and it fell even further after the offensive.

The United States was spending billions of

dollars each year to support the war effort. The government's promises that the war would end quickly and that the United States was winning just weren't enough anymore. Many Americans were losing faith in the government's and Johnson's decisions. Mothers and fathers didn't want to send their sons and daughters to die in a war halfway around the world. Americans were beginning to view the war as the responsibility of the Vietnamese to fight. And from what they saw on television, it was an incredibly brutal war. These feelings were reflected in public opinion polls. In March 1968 only 26 percent of Americans supported President Johnson.

Then a new military request leaked to the press. In early March 1968, the public was shocked to learn that General William Westmoreland, the commander of the troops in Vietnam, wanted even more troops. He requested 206,000 more soldiers, a 40 percent increase to his forces. There were already 510,000 American troops fighting in Vietnam.

These troops would come from the draft, a system of choosing young men for required service in the military. Without enough voluntary soldiers to replace the dead and wounded, Johnson had started a draft in 1964. As many as 40,000 men were drafted each month. The year of the Tet Offensive, 1968, was one of the deadliest years of the war for the

Without enough voluntary soldiers to replace the dead and wounded, Johnson had started a draft in 1964.

Vietnam veterans as well as civilians marched to the Pentagon to protest against the war.

U.S. Close to 17,000 Americans died and 87,388 were wounded. And many more Vietnamese soldiers and civilians died or were hurt.

Many young men had been resisting the draft in public protests where they burned their draft cards. Large antiwar protests were happening around the country too. Just the year before, close to 100,000 protestors marched to Washington, D.C., to voice

their concerns about the war. Johnson denied
Westmoreland's request partly because he thought it
would spark even bigger protests. And in just a few
months, Johnson replaced Westmoreland in Vietnam.

At the end of March Johnson had come to a
decision about his future too. He and millions of
Americans had watched Cronkite's special about the
war. It bothered Johnson deeply. Cronkite was
a trusted news reporter. The president knew his
view was important to average Americans across
the country. Johnson told one of his aides,

The Vietnam War affected every American, not least of all the president.

"If I've lost Cronkite, I've lost the country."

On Sunday night, March 31, 1968, Johnson made a televised address to the nation. He began his speech by saying he wanted to talk about peace in Vietnam. He seemed tired. He spoke clearly and plainly. He described events from the Tet Offensive and how the communists had not succeeded in taking control of South Vietnam. He wanted to discuss a peace treaty with North Vietnam, and announced he would begin limiting the attacks against the North. Johnson also spoke about the United States and its people, who

were divided about the war. Then, at the end of his address, Johnson surprised the nation. He said, "I shall not seek, and I will not accept, the nomination of my party for another term as your President." Johnson, who was up for re-election, had decided he was not going to run.

Johnson's address marked the beginning of the end of U.S. involvement in the war. But the process would take another five years. With President Richard Nixon in command starting in 1969, the United States began withdrawing troops

Called the "living room war," the conflict in Vietnam was the first in history brought into people's homes through television.

and training South Vietnamese troops to take over fighting the ground war. The U.S. kept trying to negotiate a peace treaty to end the war, but the talks repeatedly failed. But on January 27, 1973, representatives from the communist North and southern forces signed a treaty with South Vietnam and the United States. The treaty, called the Paris Peace Accords, detailed the withdrawal of U.S. troops and an end to the fighting. The North agreed to release its prisoners of war. It also called for the eventual and peaceful reunification of North and South Vietnam into one country. On March 29 the final U.S. military unit left Vietnam. The United States was no longer involved in the war. It had not won its fight against communism in Vietnam.

Many believe that television, especially during the Tet Offensive, lost the war for the United States. Footage of violence and devastation entered the homes of the U.S. public on a daily basis. Called the "living room war," the conflict in Vietnam was the first in history brought into people's homes through television. Viewers saw military personnel following orders, but in missions that appeared harmful to the Vietnamese people. Villages and cities were being destroyed on camera. Viewers also saw death—of both U.S. and Vietnamese military personnel and of Vietnamese civilians. Television revealed war for what it really was, and the public reacted accordingly.

SAIGON HAS FALLEN

Desperate to leave, South Vietnamese try to scale the walls of the U.S. embassy.

The United States got out of Vietnam in 1973, but the war did not end as it was supposed to. The North still fought for control. The South Vietnamese military had more weapons and tanks, but eventually they could not fend off the North Vietnamese. In late April 1975, North Vietnamese forces were close to capturing Saigon. People had been leaving South Vietnam as fast as they could. But then the communist forces bombed the airport so no one else was able to escape.

About 1,000 Americans and thousands of Vietnamese people still wanted to leave Saigon before the communists captured the city. To get them out, the United States began Operation Frequent Wind. It would be the largest helicopter evacuation in history. It began on April 29 and went through the next morning. U.S. helicopters landed on the roofs of buildings and people clamored inside. They were desperate to leave. The helicopters brought them to 40 U.S. warships and 27 South Vietnamese ships waiting for them at sea.

Many Vietnamese people who couldn't make it onto helicopters set out to sea on rafts and small fishing boats. They hoped to get onto one of the waiting ships.

Television reports showed chaotic scenes. Crowds of people were trying to get into the U.S. embassy and onto helicopters. Many did not have the right paperwork and were turned away. Aboard the ships, South Vietnamese helicopters attempted to land on the decks. They were not familiar with landing on moving ships though. Some crashed into the sides of the ships or crash landed on deck. But there was no room for the helicopters to stay on deck. After unloading their passengers, the footage showed U.S. sailors pushing the helicopters into the sea. Other pilots dropped off their passengers, flew off to the side, and then jumped out. Their helicopters dove into the water. This evacuation of more than 7,000 people was the dramatic ending to the Vietnam War. The communists had won and television crews were there to capture the final moments.

The Three Soldiers memorial statue stands on the National Mall in Washington, D.C.

As support for the war diminished, political leaders faced limited options, and eventually the United States had to exit the conflict. Although no single factor changed public opinion toward the war, the vivid imagery left an unforgettable impression on U.S. television viewers in the 1960s and 1970s.

Timeline

May 7, 1954

The Viet Minh defeat the French at the battle of Dien Bien Phu

July 1954

Representatives from France, Vietnam, Cambodia, and Laos sign the Geneva Accords. This peace treaty temporarily splits Vietnam into two countries: North Vietnam and South Vietnam

1962

The United States has 11,326 military personnel in South Vietnam

November 1963

South Vietnam's leader Ngo Dinh Diem is assassinated on November 2 and U.S. President John F. Kennedy is assassinated on November 22. Lyndon B. Johnson becomes the new president

1956

The U.S.-backed leader of South Vietnam, Ngo Dinh Diem, refuses to hold the elections meant to unify North and South Vietnam. But the Russian- and Chinese-backed North wants the country to unify

December 20, 1960

The National Liberation Front (NLF) forms. This political organization wants to unify North and South Vietnam. Its military group is the Viet Cong

1961

Nine hundred U.S. military personnel are in South Vietnam

1963

More U.S. military personnel arrive in South Vietnam, bringing the total to 16,000

August 2–4, 1964

The Gulf of Tonkin incident happens in the South China Sea. On August 2, North Vietnamese PT boats fire upon the USS *Maddox*. On August 4, the USS *Maddox* believes it sees torpedoes on its radar system, although no enemy boats are spotted

Timeline

August 4, 1964

President Johnson announces in a televised address that the United States has begun bombing North Vietnam in response to the Gulf of Tonkin incident. It is the United State's first direct action in the war

March 8, 1965

The first U.S. combat troops arrive in South Vietnam. They include 3,500 marines

February 2, 1968

NBC News airs footage of General Nguyen Ngoc Loan executing a Viet Cong soldier. Twenty million Americans watch the brutal report on television

February 27, 1968

Walter Cronkite's hour-long special about the Tet Offensive airs on CBS. At the end of the special, Cronkite offers his opinion about the war. He believes it cannot be won, and the United States should exit the war

March 31, 1968

During a televised address, Johnson announces that the United States will start limiting its attacks against North Vietnam. Johnson also shocks the nation by saying he will not run for re-election in the upcoming presidential campaign

August 5, 1965

Morley Safer's report on the burning of Cam Ne is aired on the *CBS Evening News*. Americans are shocked to see U.S. marines burning down the homes of South Vietnamese villagers

January 30–31, 1968

The Tet Offensive begins in South Vietnam. The Viet Cong and North Vietnamese army simultaneously attack the major cities in South Vietnam

January 27, 1973

Representatives from the communist North and southern forces sign a treaty with South Vietnam and the United States to end the war

March 29, 1973

The last U.S. military unit leaves South Vietnam

April 30, 1975

The North Vietnamese Army gains control of Saigon. The Vietnam War is over and the communist North gains power, reunifying the country as one communist state

Glossary

ancestral—inherited from past relatives

antiwar—to be against a war

casualties—military personnel lost through death, injury, or capture by enemy forces

execution—act of putting someone to death

footage—a length of film made for television or movies

frontline—military lines of combat during a war

guerrilla—member of a small and independent fighting force that engages in irregular warfare, such as raids and surprise attacks, against a larger government force

infiltrated—to have gradually become established in an area for the purpose of spying on an enemy

materiel—equipment, gear, and supplies used by the military

narration—spoken commentary of a story

network—large television company that produces programs to be shown across a country

offensive—attack

resolution—formal expression of an intent that is voted upon by a group

revolutionary—relating to a movement that wants to change a society or a country

telex—communication system that sends typed messages over a telephone wire from one location to another

treaty—agreement made through negotiation

Additional Resources

Further Reading

Chant, Christopher. *Stalemate: U.S. Public Opinion of the War in Vietnam*. Broomall, Penn.: Mason Crest, 2018.

DK. *The Vietnam War: A Definitive History*. New York: DK Publishing, 2017.

Partridge, Elizabeth. *Boots on the Ground: America's War in Vietnam*. New York: Viking, published by Penguin Group, 2018.

Truong, Marcelino. *Such a Lovely Little War: Saigon 1961–1963*. Vancouver: Arsenal Pulp Press, 2016.

Internet Sites

Use FactHound to find Internet sites related to this book.
Visit *www.facthound.com*
Just type in 9780756558253 and go.

Critical Thinking Questions

American television viewers thought of Walter Cronkite as the most trusted man in America. Why do you think they thought so highly of the anchorman's opinion?

The Viet Cong soldiers were guerrilla fighters who hid from U.S. soldiers and South Vietnam's military. They did not engage in the traditional kinds of battles that U.S. soldiers were trained to fight. What challenges do you think a traditional soldier had in fighting against a guerrilla soldier during the war?

Television networks (and viewers) wanted to see the "bang-bang" footage of the Vietnam War, yet soldiers were involved in many more mundane parts of the war where they did not see action. Why do you think networks and viewers wanted to see the action on television? And how do you think that kind of coverage (rather than showing ordinary days during the war) influenced viewers?

Source Notes

p. 8, "This is what ..." Devon Ivie. "Revisit Morley Safer's Seminal Reporting From the Vietnam War." *Vulture*. http://www.vulture.com/2016/05/watch-morley-safers-report-from-vietnam.html Accessed on December 20, 2017.

p. 8, "If there were Viet Cong..." Ibid.

p. 16, "You have broader consideratons..." Dwight D. Eisenhower. "73 - The President's News Conference." April 7, 1954, *The American Presidency Project*. http://www.presidency.ucsb.edu/ws/?pid=10202 Accessed on December 20, 2017.

p. 19, "We are very anxious..." Lyndon B. Johnson. "Transcript of Television and Radio Interview Conducted by Representatives of Major Broadcast Services," March 15, 1964. *The American Presidency Project*. http://www.presidency.ucsb.edu/ws/?pid=26108 Accessed on December 20, 2017.

p. 20, "The renewed hostile actions..." Lyndon B. Johnson. "Radio and Television Report to the American People Following Renewed Aggression in the Gulf of Tonkin," August 4, 1964. Ibid. http://www.presidency.ucsb.edu/ws/?pid=26418. http://vandvreader.org/gulf-of-tonkin-resolution-4-august-1964/ Accessed on December 20, 2017.

p. 25, "American Air Force jets..." Daniel C. Hallin. *The Uncensored War: The Media and Vietnam*. Berkeley and Los Angeles: University of California Press, 1989, p. 140.

p. 28, "At the end of the day..." Bill Lenderking. "The Five O'Clock Follies." American Foreign Service Association. http://www.afsa.org/sites/default/files/vietnamReflections006.pdf Accessed on December 20, 2017.

p. 30, "Yes, we're going on..." "Reporting America at War—Morley Safer: The Burning of Cam Ne." *PBS*. http://www.pbs.org/weta/reportingamericaatwar/reporters/safer/camne.html Accessed on December 20, 2017.

p. 30, "We've had orders..." Ibid.

p. 32, "'Wait, [Can] says..." Morley Safer. *Flashbacks: On Returning to Vietnam*. New York: Random House, 1990, pp. 90-91.

p. 36, "Government troops had captured..." Chester J. Patch Jr. "And That's the Way It Was." In David Farber, ed. *The Sixties: From Memory to History*. North Carolina: The University of North Carolina Press, 1994, p. 108.

p. 38, "He called it a 'reflex photo...'" James S. Robbins. *This Time We Win: Revisiting the Tet Offensive*. New York: Encounter Books, 2010, p. 154.

p. 40, "Last week a Viet Cong suspect..." Joseph A. Palermo. *In His Own Right: The Political Odyssey of Senator Robert F. Kennedy*. New York: Columbia University Press, 2001 p.. 106.

p. 40, "The American public was utterly..." Walter Cronkite and Don Carleton. *Conversations with Cronkite*. Austin, TX: The University of Texas at Austin, 2010, p. 210.

p. 40, "Cronkite wanted..." Ibid.

p. 41, "It seems now more certain than ever..." "Final Words: Cronkite's Vietnam Commentary." *NPR*. http://www.npr.org/templates/story/story.php?storyId=106775685 Accessed on December 20, 2017.

p. 43, "I don't think I turned around..." *Conversations with Cronkite*. Austin, TX: The University of Texas at Austin, 2010, p. 213.

p. 45, "American Marines are so bogged down..." Hallin, Daniel C. *The Uncensored War: The Media and Vietnam*. Berkeley and Los Angeles: University of California Press, 1989, p. 172.

p. 47, "As bureau chief..." Ron Steinman. *A Saigon Journal: Inside Television's First War*. Columbia: University of Missouri Press, 2002, p. 34.

p. 47, "part of combat coverage..." Ibid., *p. 35.*

p. 51, "If I've lost Cronkite..." *Conversations with Cronkite*. Austin: The University of Texas at Austin, 2010, p. 213.

p. 52, "I shall not seek..." Lyndon B. Johnson: "The President's Address to the Nation Announcing Steps to Limit the War in Vietnam and Reporting His Decision Not to Seek Reelection." 31 Mar. 1968. *The American Presidency Project*. http://www.presidency.ucsb.edu/ws/?pid=28772 Accessed on December 20, 2017.

Select Bibliography

Cronkite, Walter, and Don Carleton. *Conversations with Cronkite*. Austin: The University of Texas at Austin, 2010.

Patch, Chester J. Jr. "And That's the Way It Was: The Vietnam War on Network Nightly News." In David Farber, ed. *The Sixties: From Memory to History*. North Carolina: The University of North Carolina Press, 1994.

Hallin, Daniel C. *The Uncensored War: The Media and Vietnam*. Berkeley and Los Angeles: University of California Press, 1989.

Jamieson, Neil L. *Understanding Vietnam*. Berkeley and Los Angeles: University of California Press, 1995.

Johnson, Lyndon B.: "The President's Address to the Nation Announcing Steps to Limit the War in Vietnam and Reporting His Decision Not to Seek Reelection," March 31, 1968. Gerhard Peters and John T. Woolley, *The American Presidency Project*. http://www.presidency.ucsb.edu/ws/?pid=28772 (Accessed on December 20, 2017)

MacDonald, Fred J. *Television and the Red Menace*. New York: Praeger Publishers, 1985.

Robbins, James S. *This Time We Win: Revisiting the Tet Offensive*. New York: Encounter Books, 2010.

Rottman, Gordon L. *Vietnam Infantry Tactics*. New York: Bloomsbury, 2013.

Safer, Morley. *Flashbacks: On Returning to Vietnam*. New York: Random House, 1990.

Steinman, Ron. *A Saigon Journal: Inside Television's First War*. Columbia: University of Missouri Press, 2002.

Index

About the Author

Karen Latchana Kenney is an author and editor originally from Guyana, in South America. She has written books about World War I, the Vietnam War, Japanese American internment camps, and life in a war zone. She lives in Minneapolis, Minnesota, with her family.